SUPERCROC

AND THE ORIGIN OF CROCODILES

By Christopher Sloan
Introduction by Dr. Paul Sereno

Staff for this book

Nancy Laties Feresten
*Vice President
Editor-in-Chief, Children's Books
Project Editor*

Jo H. Tunstall
Assistant Editor

Bea Jackson
Art Director, Children's Books

Lewis R. Bassford
Production Manager

Vincent P. Ryan
Manufacturing Manager

Anne Marie Houppert
Indexer

Design by Christopher Sloan

Principal consultants

Dr. Christopher Brochu
University of Iowa

Dr. James Clark
*George Washington
University*

Dr. Kevin Padian
*University of California
Museum of Paleontology,
Berkeley*

Dr. Hans-Dieter Sues
Royal Ontario Museum

**Library of Congress
Catalog-in-Publication Data**

Sloan, Christopher.
SuperCroc and the origin of
crocodiles / by Christopher
Sloan; introduction by Paul
Sereno.
p. cm.
Includes index.

Summary: Discusses prehistoric
crocodiles, including the
discovery of SuperCroc in the
Sahara Desert, and the
lifestyles, habitats, and
conservation of modern
crocodiles.
ISBN 0-7922-6691-9
(Hardcover)
1. Crocodiles, Fossil—Juvenile
literature. [Crocodiles, Fossil. 2.
Crocodiles.] I. Title.
QE892.C8 S57 2002
567.9'8—dc21
2001003976

Printed in the U.S.A.

Above: *Near the 125-million-year-old ancient lake site of Las Hoyas in Spain, a huge croc called Goniopholis lunges at dinosaurs, while others of its kind bask on the shore in the background. Amid the tree debris at right are two other crocs that lived there. One is a close relative of living croc groups and the other, shown eating an insect, is a more distant relative.*

Cover: *SuperCroc rears its head in challenge as a carnivorous dinosaur, Suchomimus, comes too close.*

Title page:
An Indopacific crocodile

Contents

Introduction

You may think that once you've seen one crocodile-like creature—or croc—you've seen them all, but peering back to the dinosaur era may shatter your whole idea of what makes a croc. SuperCroc, for example, was twice as long and many times heavier than any croc living today. It dined on dinosaurs while dwarf crocs burrowed into the mud nearby, dining on insects and snails. There were lanky crocs that could gallop on land and marine crocs with fins and paddles they used for cruising the open ocean.

Today, all crocs are restricted to the rivers, marshes, and nearshore areas of

Crocs like this one named Gomek, a wild Indopacific crocodile caught in Papua New Guinea, are reminders of what formidable creatures crocs have been throughout their history on Earth. Yet, he also reminds us of how vulnerable crocs now are to humans.

Earth's tropics and subtropics. There, equipped with hearts and lungs that allow long underwater excursions, they specialize in sneak attacks. From watery hiding places, crocs lunge suddenly and violently with open jaws toward unsuspecting prey. Once trapped in their jaws, most prey are doomed. Although living crocs are not as large as SuperCroc, their jaws are still the most powerful of any predators prowling land or river today.

This book will take you on a fascinating tour of the wild and scaly origins of crocodiles. Their story, which unfolds over more than 200 million years, is a dramatic tale of survival in the face of voracious dinosaurs, titanic asteroids, and ruthless human hunters.

Dr. Paul Sereno
March 2001

LOST WORLD OF SUPERCROC

In the middle of the Ténéré desert, whose name means "nothing," are crocs of all sizes. Among them is SuperCroc—one of the biggest types of croc ever to have lived on Earth. Once crocs swam here in deep rivers and lakes that cut across a forested plain, but now they are just bones that lie scattered in the sand of this sub-Saharan desert of Niger.

Sandblasted out of rocks in the region called Gadoufaoua, these bones have a story to tell. They are fossils—traces of a lost world preserved in the Earth. They help us imagine what this sandy area was like 110 million years ago, when plants grew everywhere and giant reptiles roamed the banks of broad rivers.

It's not easy to search this desert boneyard. You need to brave an environment with 125°F heat, sandstorms, and no water for miles around. Yet Paul Sereno, from the University of Chicago, did just that as part of a series of expeditions starting in 1993.

Sereno knew that French scientists roamed the Sahara desert as early as the 1940s collecting specimens of exotic dinosaurs and huge crocs. One scientist, Albert-Félix de Lapparent, did some of his exploring in Niger on the back of a camel. He found an assortment of croc remains, including gigantic teeth.

Then, in the 1960s, geologists working in Niger told another French paleontologist, Philippe Taquet, of a very large croc skull found

Windswept fossil jaws of a giant croc lie in the sands of Niger's desert in the region called Gadoufaoua, where Sereno's team found this specimen, as well as several other crocs new to science.

	MESOZOIC ERA	**SuperCroc's time**		CENOZOIC ERA
248 Triassic 206	Jurassic 144	Cretaceous	65	Present

Millions of years ago

Sereno (center) and other members of his expedition team scout the horizon for promising places to prospect for fossils. Despite the obstacles, such as scorching heat and lack of water, Sereno's group was able to bring 20 tons of fossils out of Niger's desert to be studied and eventually displayed in museums there.

in the desert sandstone of Gadoufaoua. Taquet inspected the skull and had it shipped to Paris. There, he and his collaborator, France de Broin, studied it before returning it to a museum in Niger. Together, they recognized that this enormous skull and the bits collected by Lapparent were from the same species. To this creature they gave the name *Sarcosuchus imperator*, meaning "flesh crocodile emperor." With a skull more than five feet long and an estimated body length of 36 feet, it was clear that *Sarcosuchus* was a giant—a croc that could only be called SuperCroc!

When Sereno set off in 1993, his plans were to search broad areas of the desert starting from where the French scientists had left off. He knew other promising fossil sites might still be out there. Sereno's return to Niger in 1997 proved him right. The expedition collected tons of fossil material, including previously unknown dinosaurs and a beautiful new six-foot-long SuperCroc skull.

The Gadoufaoua area was so rich Sereno planned a return trip for the fall of 2000. This time he brought with him five Land Rovers, collapsible containers that held 800 gallons of water each, five tons of plaster, and a team of experienced field workers. It was an expedition capable of roaming the desert for four months.

Major expeditions, however, usually involve major headaches—and the Sereno team ran into its share. The expedition's main cargo—which included its water containers—was delayed by truck breakdowns, a gas shortage, and a trucker strike. These delays forced the team to break into two groups. One team waited for the cargo in Niamey, the capital of Niger. The other team proceeded with Sereno to Agadez, an oasis town 140 miles from the first planned camp in the region of Gadoufaoua.

On reaching Agadez, Sereno and his team searched for alternative water containers. They purchased every water bottle, can, and jug they could find. It wasn't long before they were ready to charge into the desert with as much water as they could gather—a mere four-day supply.

Local guides named Hima and Bido, who knew the desert well, led the team east toward Gadoufaoua. Even though the expedition knew its ultimate destination, choosing the route was critical. The guides' desert experience helped the team navigate the maze of dunes, fields of fine sand, and gravel plains that lay between them and their destination. Even with this help, there was nothing the team could do to keep the heavily packed Land Rovers from getting stuck many times in the hot, desert sand. What is normally a six-hour ride turned to 14 hours of grueling work digging trucks out of the sand.

On their arrival at Gadoufaoua the first task was to dig further at areas they had visited on the 1997 trip. Finding these sites was difficult because shifting sand had rearranged the appearance of the area. Among the sites they searched for was one they had found earlier where the massive skull of an adult croc was lying nose-to-nose with the skull of a younger one. Soon they found it, the large croc easily

A convoy of expedition Land Rovers stretches down a rocky slope in the desert badlands. The heavily loaded trucks were often stuck in sand.

recognized by its huge set of jaws, which lay exposed in the sand.

As the excavating team began to dig, they realized that the large croc's head was separated from its own neck. Much of the rest of its body was still buried in the hill! Continued digging revealed 25 vertebrae and many other parts of the large croc's body. Sereno estimates this giant would have been 35 to 40 feet long.

The expedition team begins to extract the skulls of two giant crocs—an adult and a young one—found facing each other in the sandstone (right). A trench has been dug all around the specimens. Now a tunnel is dug underneath. Next, cloth soaked in plaster will be wrapped around the fossils to prevent them from breaking apart. Finally, they will be lifted out in blocks for a safe trip to a laboratory for study.

Above, shown at actual size, is one of SuperCroc's bony scutes, part of the armor on the croc's back. Some scutes were more than twice this size.

SuperCroc inhabited the watery environments of Niger approximately 110 million years ago during the Middle Cretaceous period. It shared this habitat with other crocs, turtles, large fish, and dinosaurs. Here, SuperCroc faces off against Suchomimus, an unusual dinosaur with a crocodile-like mouth that probably competed with SuperCroc for large fish and other prey.

SuperCroc was apparently common in ancient North Africa, based on the number of *Sarcosuchus* fossils Sereno's team and French scientists found there. Isolated teeth and croc scutes found in Brazil may be from *Sarcosuchus* or a close relative. During SuperCroc's time, Africa and South America—both of which had been part of the ancient supercontinent Gondwana—were still joined together in the north. This connection allowed some crocs, and possibly SuperCroc, to travel between the continents.

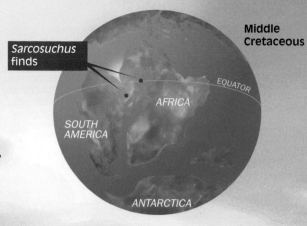

Middle Cretaceous

Sarcosuchus finds

EQUATOR

AFRICA

SOUTH AMERICA

ANTARCTICA

Paul Sereno brushes sand from a newly discovered croc nicknamed "sabercroc" for its dagger-like front teeth. It was one of several fossil crocs discovered in the Gadoufaoua region that are completely new to science. Among them is a blunt-snouted croc with a duck-like appearance (below) that in life was probably no more than three feet long.

The size confirmed Taquet's earlier estimates. SuperCroc is almost twice as long as the largest crocs living today.

Although water was still a problem, team members worked daily in the hot sun. Water was rationed both for drinking and for mixing plaster. Without plaster, the team could not make the "jackets" that are wrapped around fossils to protect them when they are moved from the field. It was grueling work, but the excitement of discovery in the rich fossil beds kept the team going. Each day presented the chance of discovering new species of crocs, dinosaurs, turtles, and fish. The remains of giant crocs turned out to be the most common fossils in the area. "We would literally walk over skulls," says Sereno.

In the middle of this fossil-finding frenzy, the other half of the expedition team finally arrived. With them came the long-lost cargo. The whole team now had their tools, fresh clothes, sleeping bags, good food, and, best of all, their 800-gallon water containers. They celebrated by taking showers and feasting on their new supply of dehydrated food.

In the end, the team not only uncovered eight or nine SuperCroc skulls of various sizes, but they found vertebrae, limb bones, and many one-foot-wide bony armor plates—called scutes—from the giant crocs as well. The new material from these *Sarcosuchus* specimens will help scientists understand more about the growth patterns of these amazing creatures and their relationship to other crocs.

From their work in the Gadoufaoua region and several other sites in Niger, the expedition collected over 20 tons of fossils. This included several new crocs, as many as

Like a patient at a dentist, SuperCroc's massive mouth is open to a technician who carefully drills bits of sandstone away from teeth and bone. It will take months of patient work at this University of Chicago laboratory to remove all the Sarcosuchus *and other fossils from their plaster jackets and get them ready for study and display.*

a dozen new dinosaurs, and many other fossils, including plants. These finds helped Sereno understand more about the ancient animals and environment in this region.

Sereno describes the area as one that long ago had flat plains cut through by a multitude of rivers, lakes, and streams. The banks of these waterways were lush with vegetation. Turtles basked on floating logs as huge fish swam lazily beneath them. On the shore, small crocodiles and dog-size dinosaurs competed for food, while large predatory dinosaurs such as *Suchomimus* hunted larger prey. In the water—perhaps waiting for a small dinosaur to come a little closer for a drink—was SuperCroc, which, with its enormous size, was easily a match for anything on land.

For such a watery environment bursting with life to have once existed in what is now one of the most inhospitable deserts on Earth is truly a marvel of nature. It must have been ideal for SuperCroc and the other creatures of that long-lost world.

WHAT IS A CROC, ANYWAY?

Crocs are often called "living fossils" because of their long history on Earth. Although they have early origins, they are far from primitive. In fact, they are one of the most successful vertebrates ever to live on Earth.

Since the first crocs evolved 230 million years ago, they have experimented with many different body sizes, food preferences, habitats, and behaviors, but they have always been more or less the same shape. Crocs have always had long armored bodies, powerful tails, and very toothy snouts. Like their reptile cousins, turtles and lizards, crocs have a body plan that has worked well for a very long time.

Yet what exactly is a croc? The word "crocodile" comes from the Greek word *krokodeilos*, meaning "lizard." Even though crocs, with their short legs, low-hung bodies, and long tails, look a lot like overgrown lizards, they are more closely related to birds. Living crocs and birds share many physical features, such as a four-chambered heart, an air sac system in the skull, and a muscular gizzard to help digestion. Much of their behavior is also similar. Both build nests and care for their young. Even the way yolk is deposited in their eggs is the same.

To better understand the close connection between crocs and birds, we need to look closely at reptiles in the Triassic period. Living then was a group of reptiles called archosaurs, meaning "ruling reptiles." They ran, crawled, swam, and flew in almost every corner of the planet. All crocs, dinosaurs, and even flying reptiles, called pterosaurs, are archosaurs because they evolved from archosaurian ancestors during the Triassic. Birds are archosaurs, too, since they descended from dinosaurs.

Crocs and birds are the only archosaurs living today. They are at different ends of the archosaur spectrum, however, because crocs are a much more ancient group than birds. This fact gives scientists a kind of

Turtles and crocs belong to ancient groups of reptiles that have inhabited Earth's freshwater environments for hundreds of millions of years. Turtles, however, are not archosaurs.

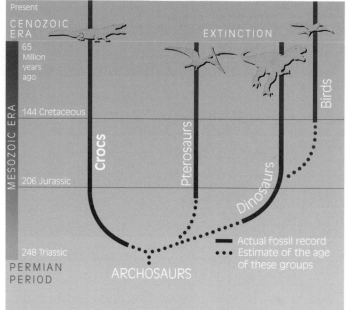

Present			
CENOZOIC ERA		EXTINCTION	
65 Million years ago			Birds
144 Cretaceous			
MESOZOIC ERA	Crocs	Pterosaurs	Dinosaurs
206 Jurassic			
248 Triassic			
PERMIAN PERIOD		ARCHOSAURS	

—— Actual fossil record
••••• Estimate of the age of these groups

Croc Origins

All crocs are archosaurs, a group of reptiles that evolved late in the Permian period. Pterosaurs and dinosaurs, including birds, are archosaurs as well. Crocs and birds are the only surviving members of this ancient group.

One feature all archosaur groups have in common is an opening in the skull in front of each eye. In early crocs, such as Protosuchus *shown below, this opening was clearly visible. In modern crocs, however, this opening has closed, possibly to strengthen the skull.*

Protosuchus, an early croc, showing the archosaurian opening (circled in red) in front of the eye

Indopacific crocodile, a living croc with no opening in front of the eye

evolutionary sandwich with birds on the top and crocs on the bottom. By studying living crocs and birds, they can learn what pterosaurs and extinct dinosaurs may have been like.

Today, crocs are the top predators in Earth's warm freshwater habitats. They live in virtually every kind of freshwater environment in the tropics and subtropics—and some nearshore saltwater habitats as well. These include marshes, mangroves, rivers, lakes, lagoons, and streams. While they lived in these environments over millions of years, crocs evolved physical features—or traits—that set them apart from other creatures.

One such trait is the croc circulatory system, which includes the croc heart, veins, arteries, and blood. No other living reptile has a heart like a croc heart. It has four chambers, as do human and bird hearts, but, unlike any other hearts, the croc heart has a valve that lets crocs control the flow of blood to their organs. This allows them to direct oxygen to the brain and heart, where it is needed most during dives that can last several hours. Their blood helps crocs stay underwater as well. Its unique chemistry allows them to get more oxygen out of a breath of air than any other creature.

Crocs are distinguished from other reptiles by their hearing, which is much better than other reptiles'. In fact, their hearing is similar to that of mammals and

Scientists reassemble the skeleton of a crocodile-like reptile called a phytosaur discovered in the Petrified Forest National Park in Arizona. No one knows why these huge crocs became extinct at the end of the Triassic period.

birds. Perhaps this explains why crocs, unlike other reptiles, have social behavior that is organized around sound. For example, mother alligators bury their eggs deep in a nest of dirt and vegetation. When baby alligators are ready to hatch from their eggs, they make grunting noises. On hearing them, the mother, who has been guarding the nest for 65 days, tears the nest open and carries the hatchlings in her mouth to the water. She will continue to protect her young for weeks, listening carefully to their calls. In some cases, they will stay together for years.

Another amazing thing about crocs was learned by studying the temperature of alligator nests. In 1982, scientists Mark Ferguson and Ted Joanen showed that, as with turtles, the sex of alligator hatchlings is determined by how warm their nests are. The scientists found that sex is determined between seven and 21 days after eggs are laid. If during this time the temperature is lower than 86°F (30°C) the hatchlings will be female. If the temperature is higher than 93.2°F (34°C) they will be male.

Many other studies have shown croc biology is tightly controlled by temperature.

CROCODILE-LIKE REPTILES

Rauisuchians and Poposaurs
Postosuchus
Triassic

Protosuchians
Triassic and Jurassic
Protosuchus
Jurassic

Phytosaurs
Rutiodon
Triassic

Aetosaurs
Stagonolepis
Triassic

Sphenosuchians
Terrestrisuchus
Triassic to Jurassic

THE CROCODYLIFORMS

Metriorhynchids
Geosaurus
Jurassic to Cretaceous

Simosuchus
Cretaceous

Croc World

In the course of their 230-million-year history on Earth, crocs have experimented with many different sizes, environments, and behaviors. Through all these experiments, however, crocs have never changed their basic body plan.

Crocs have ranged in size from the two-foot-long *Terrestrisuchus* to 40-foot-long monsters like SuperCroc. While most crocs have not been as big as SuperCroc, they have always been the largest predators in their freshwater habitats.

Yet some crocs left freshwater. The teleosaurids and metriorhynchids adapted to life in the ocean. Other crocs, such as the sebecids and pristichampsids, lived as land-dwelling—or "terrestrial"—carnivores.

Still others experimented with food. *Hylaeochampsa* and *Bernissartia* had clam-crushing teeth, and the aetosaurs and burrowing *Simosuchus* may have been plant-eaters.

LIVING CROCS

Alligators
Alligator mississippiensis
Originated 15 million years ago

Gharials
Gavialis gangeticus
Probably originated
ten million years ago

Crocodiles
Crocodylus porosus
Originated between five and
ten million years ago

Teleosaurids
Teleosaurus
Jurassic to Cretaceous

Bernissartia
Cretaceous

Hylaeochampsa
Cretaceous

Sebecids
Sebecus
Cenozoic

Pristichampsids
Pristichampsus
Cenozoic

SuperCroc
Pholidosaurs
Sarcosuchus imperator
Cretaceous

SCALE
ONE FOOT

21

Crocs make noises to defend territory, attract mates, find hatchlings, and maintain contact with each other. Young crocs, such as these alligators taking a rest on their mother, communicate frequently with their mother using grunts and squeaks. Adult crocs bark, hiss, growl, bellow, and roar. An alligator bellow can be almost as loud as a small airplane and, by slapping their jaws into the water, they can make popping noises that can sound like gunshots.

Crocs, like snakes, lizards, and turtles, are "cold-blooded." Their blood is not actually cold, but unlike mammals, a croc's body temperature depends on the temperature of the air, ground, or water around it. Although crocs can withstand temperature extremes—even freezing temperatures—they prefer areas where the coldest day does not go below 50°F. In today's climate, this means crocs generally live near the Equator.

Their cold-blooded biology is one reason crocs like SuperCroc got so big. Crocs do not have to use energy to keep their bodies warm, as warm-blooded animals do. This allows them to convert more of the food they eat into stored energy in the form of fat. Using these fat reserves, large crocs can go as long as two years without eating! If, on the other hand, food is plentiful, crocs can devote energy to building bone and muscle. Under these circumstances, some species of crocs are able to grow as much as 1.5 feet per year. Once they reach adulthood, which varies between species, their growth slows.

The largest living croc—and the largest living reptile—is the Indopacific crocodile, which is also known as the saltwater or estuarine crocodile. This crocodile, which inhabits

Snout Doubt

Living crocs fall into three groups: crocodiles, alligators, and gharials. Although the word "crocodile" is often used to describe all of these animals—as well as extinct crocs—the only true crocodiles are species within the genus *Crocodylus*. Likewise, the only true alligators are in the genus *Alligator*. In addition to the true crocodiles and alligators, there are another seven or so species of living crocs closely related to them.

Gharials used to be widespread, but their range is now limited to parts of Asia.

There is only one kind of gharial living today, but there is debate among scientists about whether some gharial-like crocs, including one called the "false gharial," are more closely related to crocodiles or gharials. Aside from these cases, gharials are easy to tell apart from both alligators and crocodiles because they have a long, narrow snout well adapted for catching fish. This narrow snout makes it easy for gharials to move their mouths sideways through the water without meeting as much resistance as the broader snouts of other crocs do.

Indopacific crocodiles range from India to Australia and some Pacific islands.

Distinguishing crocodiles from alligators is more complicated. There are two features that help us tell them apart—snouts and teeth. The crocodile snout is shaped like a narrow cone in most species, and the alligator snout is broad and flat. This rule works well in the United States where there is only one living species each of alligator and crocodile. Here, the broad snouts of American alligators are easy to tell apart from the narrow noses of the crocodiles.

In other countries the difference is not as obvious. The mugger crocodiles of India, for example, have very broad snouts and look quite similar to the American alligator. On the other hand, the narrow-nosed common caiman of Central and South America, which is an alligator, can easily be mistaken for a crocodile.

The American alligator is found only in the southeastern United States.

The best way for nonexperts to tell crocodiles and alligators apart is by looking at their teeth. In crocodiles the fourth lower tooth back from the tip of the snout is enlarged and overlaps the upper jaw when the mouth is closed. In alligators, the lower teeth fit into sockets in the upper jaw, so no teeth from the lower jaw can be seen when the mouth is closed.

areas extending from India to some Pacific islands, can grow to lengths of 23 feet and can weigh over two tons.

Imagine what it takes for crocs to become truly gigantic like SuperCroc. A recent study of *Deinosuchus*, another giant croc from the Cretaceous period, showed that much of what determined its huge size was simply *time*. According to the study, *Deinosuchus* grew at rates similar to other crocs for the first ten years of life. At that point other crocs reached their adult sizes, but *Deinosuchus* just kept on growing. It took 35 years for *Deinosuchus* to reach adult size! Growth rings on fossil bones show that some *Deinosuchus* crocs lived to be 50 years old—much longer than other crocs live—and that growth continued until they died.

Naturally, much of what determines a croc's size—and life span—is genetic, but even with the right genes it takes ideal conditions for crocs to grow large. This means a stable environment, a warm climate, hundreds of square miles of freshwater habitat, and plentiful prey. Places like this apparently existed at many different times in prehistory, for scientists have found not only giant fossil crocs, such as SuperCroc and *Deinosuchus*, but hundreds of other prehistoric crocs of all sizes and shapes. It is clear from the fossil record that crocs grew larger and were much more common in ancient times than they are today. For much of the last 230 million years, it must have been a croc's world.

This unfortunate frog is about to become a meal for a young Nile crocodile. The jaws of crocs are not only studded with sharp teeth, but are incredibly strong, allowing crocs to hold securely onto prey.

25

ANKLES & ARMOR

THE CROCODILE-LIKE REPTILES

More than 100 million years before SuperCroc lived, Earth's first crocs were hunting prey in wetlands all over the world. Some were hulking reptiles with mouths like caves that could swallow smaller animals in one bite. Others were small predators that skittered about on land, feeding on insects and smaller reptiles. It was the Late Triassic period—the dawn of the dinosaur era—but the dinosaurs were not in charge then. Crocs ruled the world.

The Triassic was the first of the three periods that made up the Mesozoic era—the age of reptiles. The Earth was much warmer 230 million years ago than it is today, and much of it was covered with thick, evergreen forests and swampy lowlands. This warm, wet environment was perfect for crocs.

Most of the crocs that lived at this time were archosaurs that looked very much like living crocs, but because they were such distant relatives they are often called "crocodile-like reptiles." They commonly grew to large sizes and occupied habitats both in the water and on land. Even though they were only "crocodile-like," this early group of crocs shared some important features with crocs that evolved later.

Phytosaurs, for example, were very early crocodile-like reptiles and the most distantly related of this group to living crocs. Their name means "plant lizards," but they were very much meat-eaters. These creatures stalked what is now North America, India, and Europe in large numbers. Aside from their crocodile-like outward appearance, we know that phytosaurs are related to later crocs because they were the first archosaurs

A giant phytosaur snaps at a sphenosuchian—a smaller, quicker cousin. The Late Triassic world was inhabited by many different kinds of crocodile-like reptiles, all distant relatives of living crocs.

This chapter	MESOZOIC ERA				CENOZOIC ERA
248 Triassic 206	Jurassic 144		Cretaceous	65	Present

Millions of years ago

Most crocs are equally comfortable on land and in water. When swimming, their long powerful tails snake side-to-side to propel them forward and, when necessary, allow sudden bursts of speed. Along their backs are rows of armored plates called scutes. In many swimming crocs, these plates have ridges—or "keels"—that improve the croc's ability to move in water.

to have a primitive form of a crocodile ankle. This ankle involves a peg-and-socket, movable joint that allows great flexibility in the ankle joint. It is a trait that other archosaurs do not have, but that all crocs have shared.

It is easy to tell a phytosaur from other crocs by looking at the position of their nostrils. The nostrils of phytosaurs are at the back of the snout near the eyes. The nostrils were usually the highest point on their skulls and probably worked like a snorkel, allowing them to breathe while the rest of the head was underwater. All other groups of crocs have nostrils at the front end of their snouts. This allowed them to float in the water with only their nostrils and eyes exposed.

Many archosaurs had suits of armor, and the crocodile-like reptiles were no exception.

Crocodilo-what?

Hundreds of reptilian species related to living crocs have lived on Earth, all with the basic croc body plan. Just as scientists group living crocs by traits, they organize extinct forms by these physical features as well. As scientists change the way they think about croc evolution, the members of groups change and so do the group names. Here are some of the current groups.

The whole crocodile line, including phytosaurs, is a large group linked by their unique ankles. This group is called the "Crocodylotarsi," meaning "crocodile-ankles." This one trait—the design of their ankle bones—is distinct enough to connect all crocs through all their millions of years of evolution.

A group within the Crocodylotarsi is "Crocodyliformes." This group includes living as well as many extinct groups of crocs. It does not include crocodile-like reptiles. Four-toed hind feet and flat heads are just two of the many traits these animals share. When one refers to members of this group, they are called "crocodyliforms," spelled without an "e."

Another important group is the "Crocodylia." Crocodylians include all living crocs and all extinct descendants of their common ancestor. No one knows what that ancestor was, but it was probably similar in appearance to living crocs.

The word "crocodilian" with an "i" is also used, but not by scientists who study relationships among crocs. It comes from the word "Crocodilia," which is a group name no longer used by scientists. This means that "crocodilian" is a vague and confusing term scientifically.

In this book we use the scientific names of groups when it is helpful to point out differences. Otherwise we use the word "croc" to describe all crocodiles and crocodile-like creatures.

An eight-inch-long fossil crocodyliform from Spain

Aetosaurs, such as this Late Triassic Longosuchus *found in Texas (below), were covered in elaborate suits of armor. This defense may have been necessary to protect them from their carnivorous cousins, the phytosaurs (right). Some phytosaurs grew twice as big as aetosaurs and probably preyed on anything they could grab and hold on to.*

The throats, bellies, and backs of phytosaurs, for example, were covered by a thick bony shield. This body armor, which almost all crocs since have shared, was made of dozens of bone scutes lying within skin that was covered by horny scales. It protected crocs from attack and from being injured while they were struggling with prey.

One group of crocodile-like reptiles, the aetosaurs, were more heavily armored than any of their croc cousins. Their large bodies were not only covered with armor, but bony plates jutted out from their backs as long rows of sharp blades. They looked like reptilian armadillos. These heavily armored crocs needed protection because they were among the

few archosaurs that were not carnivorous. The shape of their teeth suggests that most aetosaurs were peaceful plant-eaters.

And indeed there were some fierce creatures to defend against. Aside from the phytosaurs, which probably lived in swamps, there were equally scary predatory crocs on land. These were the rauisuchians and poposaurs, some of which grew to be 20 feet long. They had serrated teeth similar to those of dinosaurs like *Tyrannosaurus rex*. These allowed them to kill by tearing chunks of flesh from their prey. Rauisuchians and poposaurs probably hunted and scavenged as carnivorous dinosaurs did millions of years later.

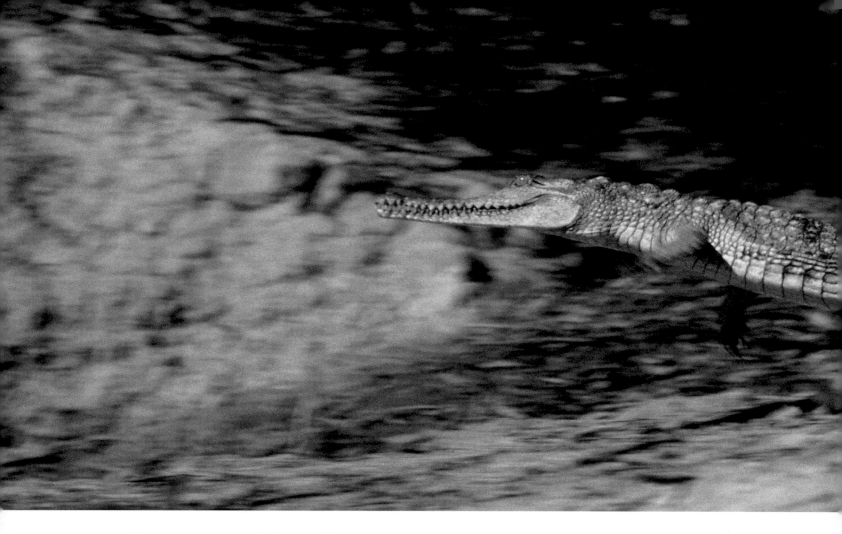

Darting among the legs of these large crocs were a number of small crocodile-like reptiles called sphenosuchians. *Terrestrisuchus*, for example, was a very long-legged sphenosuchian with a thin whip of a tail, but it did not stretch even two feet from its nose to the tip of its tail. Its light build and long legs suggest it could run very fast on land. These small terrestrial crocs probably looked more like greyhounds than crocodiles.

These days, you aren't likely to see any crocs sprinting through the forest like *Terrestrisuchus* did, but living crocs are still capable of moving very fast. They can do this on land in several ways. They can slither quickly on their bellies or lift themselves up to do a rapid "high walk." Some crocs can even gallop.

During a high walk, crocs carry their bellies well off the ground while their legs are more or less beneath their bodies. This style of walking is probably the way most ancient crocs walked and ran. Sprawling with bellies on the ground and legs out to the side, on the other hand, is a relatively new posture for crocs. It is made possible by changes in the ankle and leg bones of modern crocs.

Of all these high-walking crocs that dominated both the freshwater and land habitats in the Late Triassic, only the small terrestrial crocs survived into the period that followed—the Jurassic. Among them were the protosuchians—the first members of a whole new group of crocs that were different from the crocodile-like reptiles. It was from these tiny crocs—not the fierce crocodile-like reptiles—that all later groups, including the one that produced SuperCroc, evolved.

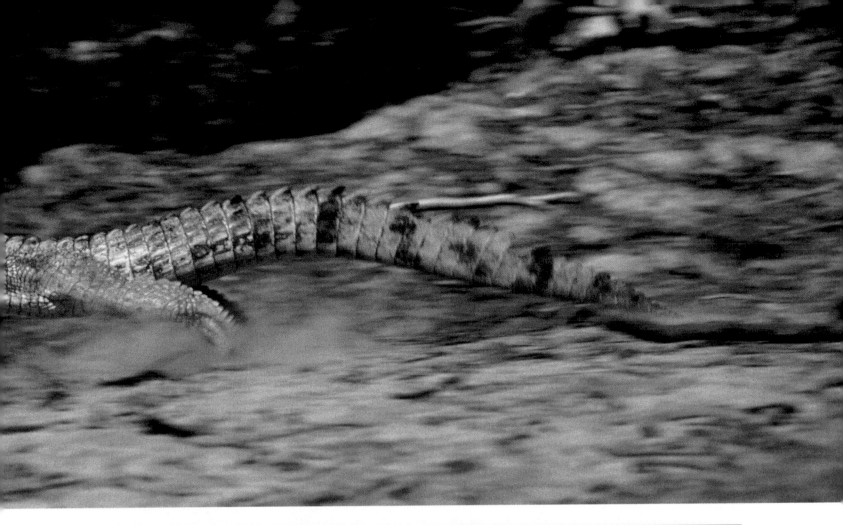

Galloping freshwater crocs from Australia, like this one rocketing toward water (top), have been clocked at 18 miles per hour. This behavior is probably very similar to that of the small Triassic crocs that galloped through the end of the Triassic period and into the Jurassic. Yet quick crocs like the sphenosuchian Hesperosuchus (above foreground) were not the only archosaurs to survive. Small dinosaurs similar to Coelophysis, shown here in the background, did as well.

MONSTERS & MIDGETS

THE CROCODYLIFORMS

On a wintry day in New York City in 1940, a huge crate arrived at the American Museum of Natural History in New York City. Paleontologist Barnum Brown looked at the box he had packed two weeks earlier with his colleague R.T. Bird. The crate held a huge block of stone that Brown hoped contained the remaining parts of a large croc he had discovered in the Big Bend area of west Texas. As he and Bird prepared to open it, Brown remarked, "We ought to see if we have anything worthwhile."

Bird's job was to tease the bones carefully out of the rock. The stone seemed hard as iron, and it was a full week before something like a croc hip bone started to emerge. One day, to Bird's immense surprise, his chisel cut into what could only be a tooth socket. When Brown saw this he declared, "No, it can't be!" What they had thought was a hip bone was actually a part of the skull of the largest crocodile yet discovered, *Deinosuchus*.

Estimated to be 30 to 35 feet long, *Deinosuchus*—terror crocodile—was nearly as long as *Tyrannosaurus rex*. Like SuperCroc in ancient Africa, *Deinosuchus* lived during the Cretaceous period in North America when large carnivorous dinosaurs prowled the land. In fact, *Deinosuchus* may have competed directly with *T. rex* for prey because their ranges overlapped. Both giants may have been on the lookout for meals of prey such as duck-billed dinosaurs or carcasses. Much had happened since the end of the Triassic period when the only crocs left were relatively small.

At the beginning of the Jurassic, the period that followed the Triassic, the smaller terrestrial crocs and dinosaurs had a more or less even playing

Deinosuchus *was a giant croc that lived among—and probably fed on—dinosaurs like the duckbills in this scene. It inhabited many parts of North America during the Cretaceous period.*

MESOZOIC ERA	This chapter				CENOZOIC ERA
248 Triassic 206	Jurassic	144	Cretaceous	65	Present

Millions of years ago

The gape of a caiman shows how a flap of skin at the back of the mouth can prevent water from entering its throat when it opens its mouth underwater. Internal nostrils, located in the throat behind this flap, allow it to breathe when the flap is closed.

field on land. As dinosaurs became more common on land, however, terrestrial crocs grew more scarce. Either group could have evolved to become the dominant land vertebrates at that time, but apparently the dinosaurs were more successful competitors. No one knows for sure what edge the dinosaurs had, but one possibility is that they gained some advantage because they ran on two legs. Perhaps this made them faster or better at maneuvering on land than four-legged crocs.

Crocs may have been crowded off the land, but the disappearance of phytosaurs and other large crocodile-like reptiles at the end of the Triassic left a vacancy for big predators in freshwater habitats. It wasn't long before Jurassic crocs moved into those areas. There, they became so effective as aquatic predators that they never left that role, and no other animal has ever been able to dislodge them.

From this base as freshwater predators, crocs did much experimenting to compete and survive throughout the rest of the Mesozoic era and into the Cenozoic era—the age

Post-Nasal Drift

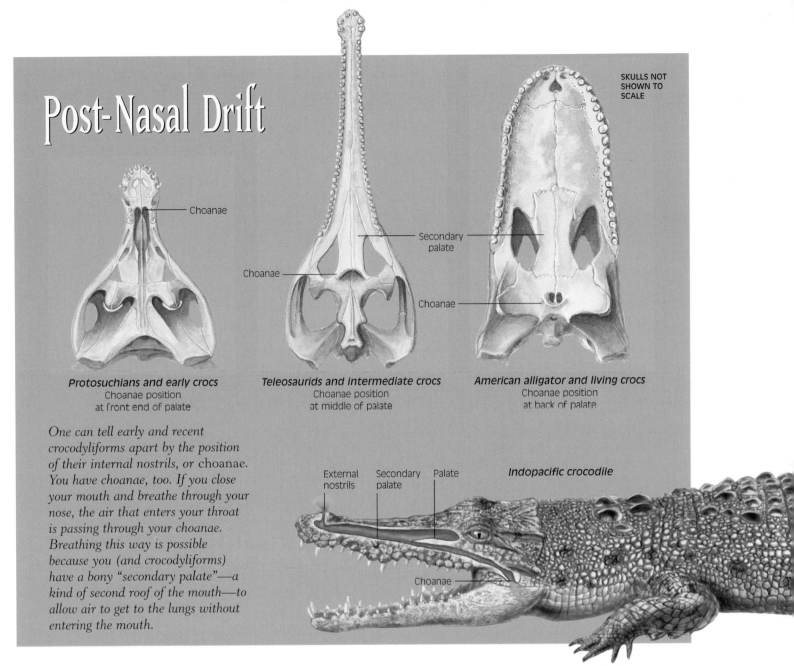

Choanae

Secondary palate

Choanae

Choanae

Protosuchians and early crocs
Choanae position at front end of palate

Teleosaurids and intermediate crocs
Choanae position at middle of palate

American alligator and living crocs
Choanae position at back of palate

One can tell early and recent crocodyliforms apart by the position of their internal nostrils, or choanae. You have choanae, too. If you close your mouth and breathe through your nose, the air that enters your throat is passing through your choanae. Breathing this way is possible because you (and crocodyliforms) have a bony "secondary palate"—a kind of second roof of the mouth—to allow air to get to the lungs without entering the mouth.

External nostrils   Secondary palate   Palate

Indopacific crocodile

Choanae

of mammals. During the millions of years that they lived among dinosaurs and then, after the dinosaur extinction, among mammals, they tried many different habitats and behaviors. They were fish-eaters and meat-eaters, monsters and midgets, and land-dwelling as well as sea-going crocs. All of these kinds of crocs are called crocodyliforms—the "crocodile-shaped ones." Unlike crocodile-like reptiles, crocodyliforms generally have a flat head called a "skull table," a tail surrounded by small bony plates, and four instead of five toes on their hind feet.

The crocodyliforms are a very large and ancient group, making it a challenge for scientists to sort out relationships within the group. Yet, there are key differences that scientists look for that can help. For example, one can tell the difference between primitive and advanced crocodyliforms by looking at details in the skull and the shape of the vertebrae.

Inside the skull of all living crocs is an air passage that leads from the nostrils at the front end of the snout to "internal nostrils" in the throat, called the choanae (pronounced ko-WAH-nay). The choanae allow crocs—and you—to breathe while eating or when the mouth is underwater.

The position of the choanae of crocodyliforms changed over time. In earlier crocodyliforms, the choanae were inside the mouth near the tip of the snout. Over tens of millions of years they shifted toward the back of the palate and eventually to their modern position in the throat. The position of the choanae and the bones surrounding them reveal how primitive or advanced a croc might be.

Vertebrae are also useful in identifying primitive or advanced crocs. The vertebrae in early crocs were only slightly curved on each end. In more advanced crocs, the vertebrae fit together like a ball-and-socket joint. When lined up, the bulge of one vertebra fits neatly into the hollow of the one next to it. This increases both strength and flexibility of the spine and tail.

In 1930 a film crew from Hollywood stumbled onto one of the earliest known crocodyliforms. While filming a Western in the beautiful Painted Desert of northern Arizona, one of the workers came across some fossil bones. Barnum Brown was contacted, and the next year he arrived in Arizona to see if he could find more of the animal. Brown unearthed the skeleton of a small creature from Early Jurassic-period sandstones. Its choanae, vertebrae, and other features clearly distinguished it from crocodile-like reptiles. It was a terrestrial croc and was named *Protosuchus*, meaning "first crocodile."

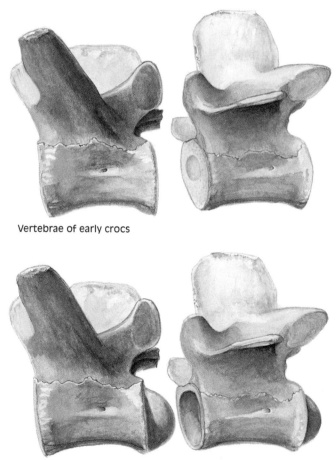

Vertebrae of early crocs

Vertebrae of more recent crocs

The vertebrae of crocs changed as they evolved from early forms to more recent ones. The ends of the vertebrae in early crocs were more or less flat. More recent crocs have a more flexible and strong connection created by a ball-and-socket joint.

Protosuchians must have been a successful group of crocs. Since the discovery of *Protosuchus* in Arizona, similar crocs have been found all around the world, including Africa, South America, and China. They have also been found in Triassic age deposits, indicating they originated then but did not become extinct as did many other crocs.

Other primitive crocodyliforms were found in Europe during the 1700s among Jurassic age rocks. They were among the first vertebrate fossils ever studied by scientists. These animals, the teleosaurids

and metrio-
rhynchids,
had more
advanced traits than *Protosuchus* and quite a
different lifestyle. These were sea-going crocs! Unlike
the *Protosuchus* bones, which were found lying near
dinosaur footprints, these fossils were found in
marine deposits among the bones of
swimming reptiles. This suggests that
these crocs competed for fish with
other large reptiles that lived in
the ocean at that time.

The most common
of these marine crocs
were the teleosaurids.
These creatures looked
very similar to living
gharials. Their long
snouts and short
forelimbs are a good
indication that they
were devoted to a life
of eating fish and
swimming.

Yet no teleosaurid
went as far as the
metriorhynchids did in
their experiment with
the salty seas. These
crocs had flippers and fins.
As they adapted to an
aquatic way of life, their
arms and legs became
flippers. They also lost
their armor in favor of
smooth swimmers'
bodies. There is even
evidence that their tails
supported a fin similar
in appearance to that
of a shark.

*Like today's gharials (inset), the metriorhynchids specialized
in catching fish with their long narrow snouts. This Late
Jurassic Geosaurus is a fossil metriorhynchid from southern
Germany. Unlike most other crocs, metriorhynchids were
totally aquatic and lived in a saltwater habitat. Their
arms and legs were flippers and, as this fossil shows,
their tails had vertical fins like shark tails.*

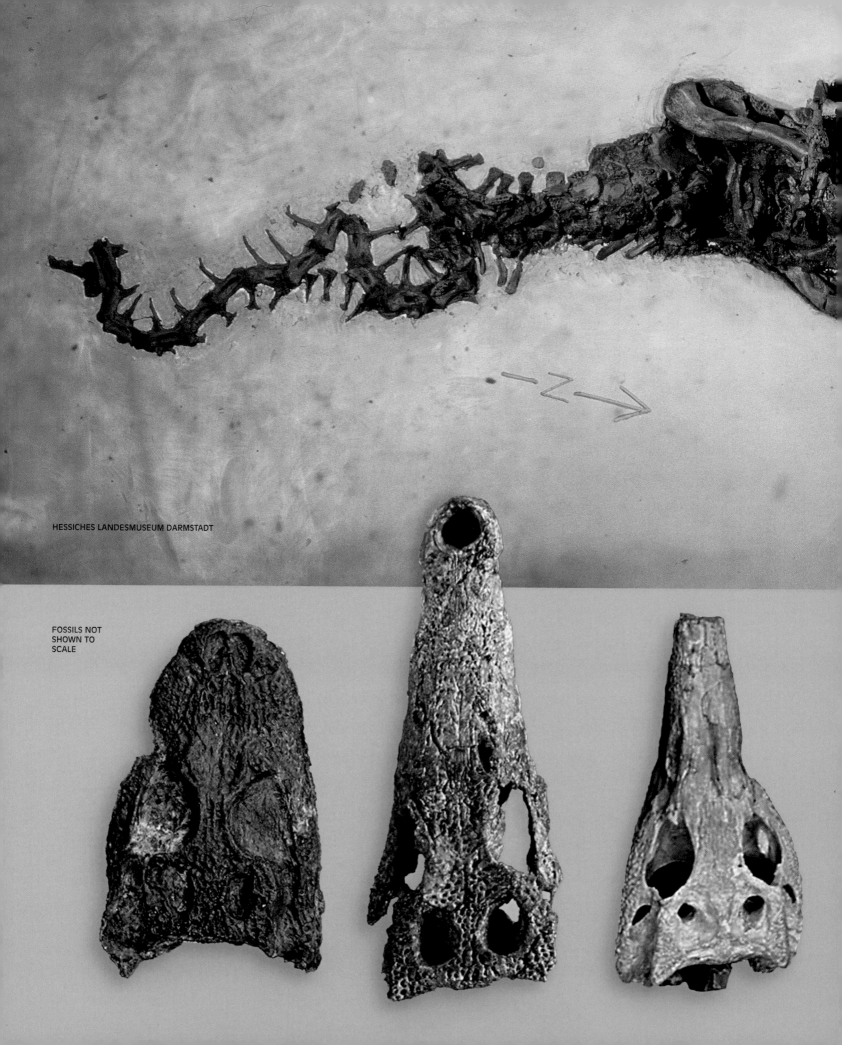

HESSICHES LANDESMUSEUM DARMSTADT

FOSSILS NOT
SHOWN TO
SCALE

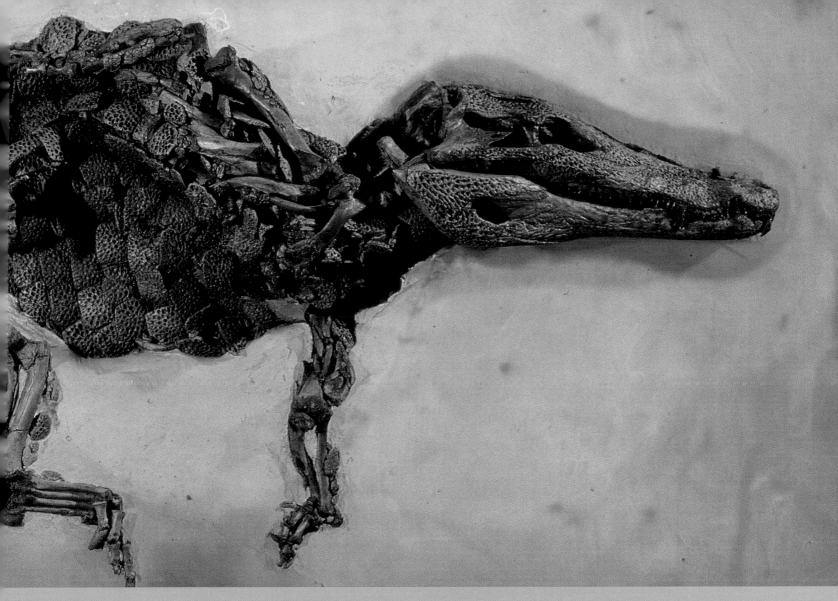

Croc Diversity

Fossil crocs come in all shapes and sizes and from all corners of the world. The 4.5-foot-long croc shown above is Diplocynodon *from Messel, a site in Germany where the preservation of 49-million-year-old fossils is exceptionally fine.*

Deinosuchus, *shown at left with the scientists who discovered and studied it, is among the largest crocs ever. Although it was first thought to be similar to a crocodile, scientists now suggest it was more like an alligator.*

China has a rich record of fossil crocs. Shown at far left, from left to right, are an early alligator, a terrestrial croc called Planocrania, *and* Hsisosuchus. *All three lived in the Jurassic period.*

Most croc teeth are conical (near right) and are designed for holding onto prey as it is torn apart or drowned. The teeth of some terrestrial crocs, such as Sebecus (above) were flattened and had serrated edges for slicing flesh—a better design for killing on land. Still other crocs had plant-eater teeth, such as those of Simosuchus (far right).

Although the appearance and behavior of these marine crocs are fascinating, most Jurassic- and Cretaceous-period crocs looked and probably behaved much like the crocs of today. Their bodies were perfect for hunting along the shores of freshwater habitats where there were plenty of fish, small dinosaurs, and later on, even mammals to munch on. SuperCroc was one of these. It was an enormous pholidosaur, another ancient group that looked a lot like gharials.

And from somewhere among these many crocodyliforms came the common ancestor of living crocs. That creature was probably not a giant, but a humble little animal similar to *Bernissartia*, an Early Cretaceous croc from Europe. Its fossilized remains were found in coal beds among the skeletons of many dinosaurs. *Bernissartia* had an advanced choanae position and hints of ball-and-socket vertebrae. It also displayed the modern croc condition of having more than two rows of back scutes.

An asteroid impact at the end of the Cretaceous may have triggered the extinction of many forms of life—including all dinosaurs except birds, but this event seems to have had little effect on crocs. No one knows for certain why—but some scientists suggest it was the freshwater habitat of crocs and their ability to survive long periods without food that saved them. They argue that many forms of flowering plants and marine plankton died out during the extinction event, and creatures that depended on these as part of their food web could have had difficulty surviving. Neither flowering plants nor marine plankton are part of the fresh water food web that many crocs depend on, however. So crocs and other freshwater creatures may have survived the extinction because their food chain was left more intact than others.

In the 65 million years since the dinosaur extinction and the end of the Mesozoic era, crocs have continued to explore a variety of lifestyles and habitats. Several groups of crocs from the era that followed, the Cenozoic, went back on shore and became terrestrial predators. Among them were a snaggletoothed monster called *Sebecus* and a strange, hoof-toed croc called *Pristichampsus*. Unlike other crocs that have conical teeth designed to catch and hold prey until it drowns or is torn apart, these crocs evolved flattened teeth with serrated edges like steak knives. This tooth design, much like that of carnivorous dinosaurs, was well suited for killing on land by slicing flesh. It is possible that these terrestrial crocs took advantage of places where there was little competition from large mammal predators. This may be why *Quinkana*, a ten-foot-long terrestrial croc, survived in Australia until as recently as 29,000 years ago.

At some points during the Cenozoic, there were many more crocs around than today, and their ranges stretched to areas of the world that are now cooler, and therefore unsuitable for crocs. Extinct relatives of gharials, for example, were once common in North America and Europe. Europe once had crocodile and alligator relatives as well. Now the ranges of these animals are reduced and climate is partly to blame. But climate is not the biggest problem facing living crocs.

Only recently, crocs have gotten into serious trouble. They've encountered new competitors that are fast, smart, and jealous of their freshwater habitat. This competition is bringing crocs closer to extinction than ever before in their 230-million-year history.

Who are these dangerous newcomers? Humans.

Iberosuchus *was a terrestrial croc related to* Sebecus. *It grew to be ten feet long and galloped around in what is now Spain 34 million years ago .*

Pristichampsus *was an unusual terrestrial croc that had hooflike toes. Here it is shown preying on dog-size early horses.* Sebecus *(below) was another terrestrial croc that, like other land-dwelling crocs, had serrated teeth set in deep jaws. Both lived in the Cenozoic era.*

Protosuchus *was a small terrestrial croc that lived in both the Triassic and Jurassic periods. It was among the earliest of the crocodyliforms.*

Crocs Everywhere

Whether on land or in the water, crocodyliforms were formidable predators. The terrestrial crocs (left), however, did not reach the huge scale of aquatic crocs, some of which were similar in size to SuperCroc. All of the crocs shown here lived at different times.

Deinosuchus (above) was a gigantic Cretaceous period croc from North America that probably fed on dinosaurs like the duckbill Corythosaurus it is shown attacking here. Purrusaurus (below) was a giant caiman—a relative of alligators—that lived in South America during the Cenozoic era. It is estimated to have grown to be more than 36 feet long.

The Puzzle of Croc Island

While scrambling around the dry hills of western Madagascar one day in 1998, croc expert Greg Buckley discovered something that he never expected to see. Buckley and Laurent Randriamiaramanana, a student from Madagascar's University of Antananarivo, were out prospecting in sandstones laid down in rivers that ran there 70 million years ago during the Late Cretaceous period. They stumbled across what appeared to be a perfectly preserved fossil of the front half of a croc. Its snout was embedded in rock so only the back of the skull was visible. It took a week to put it in a plaster jacket so it could travel safely back to Buckley's Chicago laboratory.

Back in Chicago, Buckley carefully removed the rock from the croc's skull and was surprised to find that the snout came to an abrupt end. At first he thought it was broken. As he teased more sandstone away from the bone, however, he realized that was not true. It was just a very bizarre croc! Not only did it have a very short, blunt snout, its mouth was filled with leaf-shaped teeth similar to those of plant-eating animals. He named this odd new croc *Simosuchus* and added it to the list of unexpected fossil surprises being found in Madagascar.

The blunt snout and other features of Buckley's croc showed that, like other recently found fossils, *Simosuchus* was related to crocs that lived during the Late Cretaceous period in South America. "Everything about Madagascar's Cretaceous crocs screams South America," said Buckley, but what are they doing in Madagascar?

Since 1996, paleontologist David Krause has led a team of scientists, including Buckley, on summer expeditions to Madagascar in an effort to answer that question. Any fossils they find are important clues because so little is known about ancient life there. Since they started, they have added many new animals to the island's fossil species list. They have found new dinosaurs, small reptiles, ancient birds, tiny mammals, and lots of crocs. In total, Krause's team has unearthed seven different kinds of crocs—more than any other kind of animal. They range in size from 2 to 18 feet from

In the Late Cretaceous, Madagascar's rivers and shores were teeming with crocs. This could have made it difficult for herds of dinosaurs like these titanosaurs (right) to cross rivers during the dry season when crocs would tend to be grouped close together.

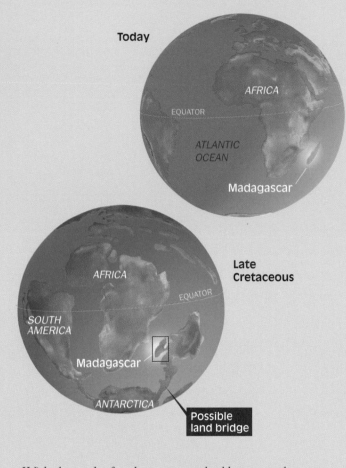

Today

AFRICA

EQUATOR

ATLANTIC
OCEAN

Madagascar

Late
Cretaceous

AFRICA

EQUATOR

SOUTH
AMERICA

Madagascar

ANTARCTICA

Possible
land bridge

*With the teeth of a plant-eater and a blunt nose that may
have been used for digging burrows, Simosuchus (right), was
one fossil croc that scientists digging in Madagascar did not
expect to find. Its features linked it to crocs that lived during
the Late Cretaceous period in South America. At that time
creatures like these might have traveled freely between
Madagascar and South America via a possible land bridge
connecting the now isolated island to Antarctica.*

the tip of its snout to the tip of its tail. Apparently Madagascar's ancient rivers and
streams were crawling with crocs! As they studied the fossils, Krause and his team
discovered some surprising information about Madagascar's past.

Many of the creatures Krause and his band of researchers found suggested
connections to South America. During much of the Cretaceous, Africa and South
America were joined as part of the ancient supercontinent, Gondwana. This allowed
many animals, possibly including SuperCroc, to travel freely between north Africa and
northern South America at that time. Madagascar, however, had broken away from the
rest of Gondwana—including Africa—millions of years earlier. By the Late Cretaceous
Madagascar had drifted hundreds of miles from Africa. Finding connections between
Madagascar's and South America's creatures so late in the Cretaceous was a surprise.

So, how did Late Cretaceous South American crocs and other animals get to
Madagascar? One could say they swam from Africa, but *Simosuchus* was most likely a
terrestrial croc and could not swim long distances. Neither could dinosaurs.

Krause's solution to this puzzle was to suggest that Madagascar stayed connected to South America through a bridge of land to Antarctica. Antarctica was in a more northerly position and had a much warmer climate then. It still maintained its Gondwanan connection to the southern tip of South America. A land bridge between Madagascar and Antarctica could have completed a route for crocs, as well as dinosaurs and other animals, to travel between the island and South America in the Late Cretaceous. Scientists who study the movement of continents have confirmed that this is possible.

Who knows what other secrets and surprises Madagascar is hiding? Each new find Krause's team makes suggests that there is much more to learn. For example, although Krause's team is finding lots of connections between Madagascar's Late Cretaceous creatures and South America, they have yet to find any connection between the fossils they find and the animals living in Madagascar today, including Madagascar's crocodiles. By digging further, scientists are sure to encounter new surprises as well as find more answers to the puzzle of croc island.

THE LAST EXTINCTION?

People and crocs are at war. At risk is the survival of the more than 20 species of crocs living today. The problem is that, at first glance, the interests of crocs and humans seem to be at odds. Humans are attracted to the same freshwater areas that attract crocs. When they get too close, there are often deadly results. Swimmers and fishermen in Australia have been killed by large Indopacific crocodiles. Nile crocodiles also have a bad reputation for snatching unwary bathers and fishermen from the shallows of the rivers and lakes of Africa.

Beyond being dangerous to humans, crocs are also seen as harmful to the efforts of fishermen. They not only compete for the fish, but interfere with nets. This has naturally created a negative feeling toward crocs among the many people who live near them. Crocs are frequently killed on sight, and their nests, when discovered, are destroyed.

It is true that crocs occasionally kill humans and interfere with human activity, but humans are far more damaging to crocs. Each year, countless acres of ideal croc habitat are destroyed by development or pollution. In addition, poachers all over the world kill thousands of crocs and smuggle their valuable skins, meat, and eggs to market.

Up until the 1970s, the demand for leather from crocodiles, alligators, and gharials, as well as the demand for their meat and eggs, drove many crocs near extinction. Gharials and American crocodiles were particularly hard hit. In that decade, scientists counted only 200 breeding-age gharials in the rivers of India, Pakistan, and Bangladesh. American crocodiles living in Florida were down to fewer than 25 nesting females.

After more than 200 million years on Earth and surviving many major extinctions, crocs are now seriously threatened by the activities of humans.

Crocs and fishermen mix with deadly results. On Lake Turkana in Kenya crocs become entangled in nets and often tear them in their struggles. They frequently drown or suffer death at the hands of angry fishermen.

International agreements to control the sale of skins, combined with local conservation efforts, modestly improved the situation for American crocodiles. In Florida, for example, the number of crocodile nests counted increased to around 100 in the year 2000. This corresponds to a population of 500 to 800 adults and a total population between 7,500 and 10,000. Some of these crocodiles are returning to areas around the Florida Keys where they had become extremely scarce. Others are thriving in new areas, like the cooling canals of a nuclear power station near Miami, Florida.

Gharials have not been so lucky. Although major conservation efforts—including complete protection, captive breeding, and restocking—brought gharials back from the brink of extinction, they are still struggling. One of the biggest problems is that there is nowhere for gharials to go on the heavily populated Indian subcontinent. Restocked gharial populations can only succeed in the most isolated stretches of protected rivers. As a result, gharial groups are small, few, and far between. This makes it difficult for them to reproduce and maintain a stable population.

In other cases, croc populations increased in response to conservation efforts. Yet this brought a new set of problems. In Australia, hunting of Indopacific crocodiles—or "salties," as they are called there—was prohibited in 1971 when the wild population was estimated at 5,000 to 10,000. Since then their numbers have exploded to somewhere in the range of 80,000 to over 110,000. This increase in the crocodile population, combined with an increase in the human population and tourism, was a recipe for frequent crocodile-human encounters. Increased croc attacks forced authorities to launch ambitious crocodile-control efforts. Through a combination of public education, patrols of harbors and rivers, relocation of problem crocodiles, and egg harvesting, their efforts seem to be working. Now signs posted near rivers and shores warning visitors of crocodile danger are a frequent site in northern Australia.

The success of croc recovery programs has made farming of crocs possible around the world. In Australia and Papua New Guinea, as well as many places in Africa, Southeast Asia, and the Americas, raising and harvesting many kinds of crocs for their skins and meat is a booming business worth hundreds of millions of dollars annually. There's even a crocodile farm in France. These efforts are called "sustainable use," because they can be continued indefinitely without putting the species involved at risk of extinction.

More and more conservationists around the world are looking for practical ways—like croc farming and tourism—to save crocs. Their goal is to show how protecting endangered animals and their environment can benefit the local community. Wildlife tourism and farmed croc products, such as leather, mean jobs and potentially millions of dollars of income for businesses and governments. This takes the poaching pressure off wild croc populations. Speaking frankly about the need to promote croc farming, conservationist Dr. James Perran Ross put it this way, "Buy a handbag and save a croc."

Conservation efforts like captive breeding and sustainable-use programs may help some crocs, but they may not be enough to prevent further extinctions. Scientists have been busy studying the populations of all crocs and have found that some are critically endangered. The Chinese alligator is in the worst shape. As of 1999, only 150 individuals were counted in a severely reduced habitat of a few square miles. The Philippine, Siamese, and Orinoco crocodiles are in danger of extinction as well.

These crocs are threatened by many things that humans do, such as net fishing and illegal hunting, but the biggest threat to them is the damage humans do to their wild habitat. Most species require hundreds of square miles of undisturbed freshwater range to maintain large populations. Drainage and infilling of wetlands and mangroves for housing and farming directly reduces the habitat available to crocs by destroying or fragmenting it. Cutting down forests also destroys croc habitat, but indirectly. The silt that washes off deforested hills builds up in rivers, slowing them down and allowing the growth of algae, which can reduce the amount of oxygen in the water. This kills fish and ruins the

This tiny gharial hatchling, part of a captive breeding program set up to save this threatened species, had to be helped out of its shell by humans.

area for crocs. Water pollution is also a form of habitat destruction that kills crocs.

Crocs are tough, yet as the population of humans increases, it is harder for them to find places where their basic needs can be met. If humans can protect more places where the temperature is croc-friendly, where food is plentiful, and where there are suitable nesting areas, crocs will be fine.

Crocs play a critical role in these habitats. Conservationists and local communities are beginning to understand that when crocs disappear from their environment, it has bad effects on the plants and animals left behind. For example, without crocs swimming in rivers, silt builds up and eventually clogs channels. Without their "gator holes"—ponds carved out in the midst of vegetation—other species have fewer places to take refuge or forage during dry spells. Crocs even help fishermen. In some places crocs prefer to eat undesirable fish that otherwise prey on commercially valuable species.

So, we are slowly discovering how crocs and humans can co-exist through experience and careful study. As we learn, we may appreciate more about their long history on Earth and their important place in nature. Perhaps we will learn enough in time to prevent the end of crocs' 230-million-year presence on Earth. Little by little we might begin to see that all crocs may be super crocs!

A tiny Indopacific crocodile floats in crystal clear water near the shore. Like other kinds of living crocs, its future is not so clear. What happens to them is largely in our hands.

Glossary

aetosaurs Triassic crocodile-like reptiles that were heavily armored and possibly plant-eaters.

archosaurs A large group of reptiles that originated late in the Permian period and dominated the Mesozoic era. During the Mesozoic they evolved into crocs, pterosaurs, and dinosaurs, including birds.

Cenozoic era Commonly called the "Age of Mammals," this era began at the end of the Mesozoic era 65 million years ago. We live in the Cenozoic era.

Cretaceous period The last period of the Mesozoic era. It lasted from 144 to 65 million years ago.

Crocodyliformes (crocodyliforms) A large group of crocs that includes protosuchians among its earliest members and living crocs as its most recent members. "Crocodyliformes" is the scientific name of the group. "Crocodyliforms" without an "e" refers to the animals in the group.

Crocodylotarsi A large group of crocs that share the trait of having crocodile ankles.

genus A group of species that are grouped together because of close similarities. The genus is the first part of a scientific name. Example: for *Crocodylus niloticus*, the genus is *Crocodylus*.

Jurassic period The second period of the Mesozoic era. It lasted from 206 to 144 million years ago.

Mesozoic era Commonly called the "Age of Reptiles," the Mesozoic lasted from 248 to 65 million years ago.

metriorhynchids Jurassic and Cretaceous period crocs adapted to life in the ocean. They had no armor but had flippers and tail fins.

Permian period The last period of the Paleozoic era. It lasted from 286 to 248 million years ago.

pholidosaurs A group of crocs that lived in the Jurassic and Cretaceous periods. They were similar in appearance to gharials.

phytosaurs A diverse group of Triassic period crocodile-like reptiles.

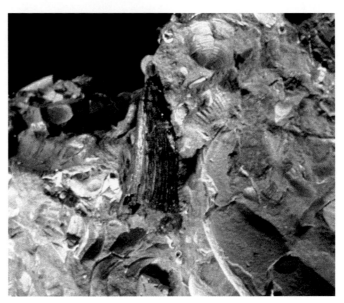

Often all that is found of ancient crocs are their teeth because they are frequently shed or broken during life. This croc tooth was found embedded among shells in Maryland.

poposaurs Large Triassic period crocodile-like carnivorous reptiles.

rauisuchians Large-skulled Triassic period crocodile-like reptiles.

Sarcosuchus A genus of giant pholidosaurs from Africa and South America.

species One kind of animal within a genus that includes closely related, similar individuals that can interbreed. The species is the second part of a scientific name. Example: For *Crocodylus niloticus*, the species is *niloticus*.

sphenosuchians Crocodile-like reptiles very closely related to, but not included among, crocodyliforms.

suchus From *souchos* or *soknopaios*—Greek words derived from the name of the Egyptian crocodile-headed god, Sobek (also Sebek).

sustainable-use The ability to use and reuse a wild renewable resource without putting it in danger of extinction.

teleosaurs Sea-going crocs from the Jurassic period with heavily armored backs and short forelimbs.

terrestrial Land-dwelling.

Triassic period The first period of the Mesozoic era. It lasted from 248 to 206 million years ago.

Index

Boldface indicates illustrations.

Acknowledgements

This book would not have been possible without the help of many generous people. My wife, Portia Sloan, in particular, deserves my thanks not only for her illustrations, but for her helpful comments on my text and page designs.

Many scientists contributed to this project with generous advice, information, and images. I would like to thank Mr. Adam Britton, Dr. Paul Willis, Dr. Gordon Grigg, Dr. Grahame Webb, Dr. Francisco Ortega, Dr. Greg Buckley, Dr. David Krause, Dr. James Perran Ross, Dr. Joe Waselewski, Dr. Zulma Gasparini, Dr. Xu Xing, Dr. Li Jinling, and Dr. Mark Norell for their help.

I would also like to thank Dr. Paul Sereno for sharing not only his sense of adventure, but information and images critical to the success of this book. Three other members of Dr. Sereno's team deserve thanks as well, Mike Hettwer for his assistance with his digital photographs from Niger, Dr. Hans Larsson for his assistance with text and artwork, and Gabrielle Lyon for her thorough Web reporting on the Niger expeditions (see www.dinosaur expedition.org).

Illustration credits

Cover: Copyright © Raul Martín. Cover flap: top, Jessica Sloan; bottom, Mike Hettwer. Endsheets: Portia Sloan; Title page: Adam Britton, Wildlife Management International. Page 2: Copyright © Raul Martín, courtesy of the Museo de las Ciencias de Castilla-La Mancha in Cuenca, Spain. Page 4: Adam Britton, Wildlife Management International. Page 6: Chris Sloan. Page 7–11: Michael Hettwer. Page 12–13: map, Chris Sloan; art © Raul Martin. Page 14–15: Michael Hettwer. Page 17: Norbert Rosing/NGS Image Collection. Page 18: top, Josh Korenblat with John Sibbick; center, Portia Sloan, courtesy of the Yale Peabody Museum; bottom, Portia Sloan. Page 19: Jonathan Blair/NGS Image Collection. Page 20–21: Portia Sloan. Page 22: Chris Johns/NGS Image Collection. Page 23: Portia Sloan. Page 24: Jonathan Blair/NGS Image Collection. Page 26: Copyright © Douglas Henderson, from *Dawn of the Dinosaurs*, by Robert A. Long and Rose Mauk, published by the Petrified Forest Museum Association, Arizona. Page 27: Chris Sloan. Page 28: Grahame Webb, Wildlife Management International. Page 29: Copyright © Raul Martín. Page 30–31: left, Neg. No 327445, courtesy Dept. of Library Services, American Museum of Natural History; right, Copyright © Douglas Henderson, from *Dawn of the Dinosaurs*, by Robert A. Long and Rose Mauk, published by the Petrified Forest Museum Association, Arizona. Page 32: Grahame Webb, Wildlife Management International. Page 33: Copyright © Douglas Henderson, from *Dinosaur Ghosts*, by J. Lynett Gillette, published by Dial, NY, NY. Page 34: Chris Sloan. Page 35: Copyright © Douglas Henderson, from *Living with Dinosaurs* by Patricia Lauber, published by Bradbury Press, NY, NY. Page 36: Joel Sartore/NGS Image Collection. Page 37: Portia Sloan. Page 38–39: top, Jonathan Blair/Hessiches Landesmuseum Darmstadt; bottom left (three images): Courtesy of Dr. Li Jinling, Institute of Vertebrate Paleontology and Paleoanthropology, Beijing; bottom right, Neg. No. 318651, courtesy Dept. of Library Services, American Museum of Natural History. Page 40: Portia Sloan. Page 41: The Natural History Museum of London Picture Library; inset: Copyright © Raghu Rai/Magnum. Page 42: Copyright © John Sibbick. Page 44: top, Mick Ellison; bottom left, Portia Sloan; bottom right: Maria Stenzel. Page 45: Copyright © Raul Martín. Page 46–47: Mark Hallett. Page 48–49: maps, Chris Sloan; Maria Stenzel. Page 50–51: Joel Sartore/NGS Image Collection. Page 52: Jonathan Blair/NGS Image Collection. Page 53: Copyright © Raghu Rai/Magnum. Page 54: David Doubilet/NGS Image Collection. Page 55: Jessica Sloan/William Atkins.

The world's largest nonprofit scientific and educational organization, the National Geographic Society was founded in 1888 "for the increase and diffusion of geographic knowledge." Fulfilling this mission, the Society educates and inspires millions everyday through magazines, books, television programs, videos, maps and atlases, research grants, the National Geographic Bee, teacher workshops, and innovative classroom materials.

See more on SuperCroc at www.nationalgeographic.com